INCREDIBLY DISGUSTING DRUGS

SPEED AND YOUR BRAIN
The Incredibly Disgusting Story

Allan B. Cobb

the rosen publishing group's
rosen central
new york

"Funded by
LSTA Young Adult Grant"

Published in 2000 by The Rosen Publishing Group, Inc.
29 East 21st Street, New York, NY 10010

Library of Congress Cataloging-in-Publication Data

Cobb, Allan B.
    Speed and your brain : the incredibly disgusting story / Allan B. Cobb.
        p. cm.—(Incredibly disgusting drugs)
    Includes bibliographical references and index.
    Summary: Discusses the nature, effects, and dangers of the drug methamphetamine, commonly known as speed, as well as treatment for addiction to it.
    ISBN 0-8239-3253-2 (lib. bdg. : alk. paper)
    1. Amphetamine abuse—Juvenile literature. [1. Amphetamines. 2. Drug abuse.] I. Title. II. Series.
    00-B6726
HV5822.A5 C63 2000
362.29'9—dc21
                                                                99-086805

Manufactured in the United States of America

CONTENTS

Introduction

Most of us know what a stimulant is: something that eliminates fatigue and excites or arouses you to greater activity. After a long, tough day at school, you may have a sugary soft drink or a candy bar or a cup of coffee to give yourself a boost of energy and to stay alert. But it's not just the sugar in soda or coffee or candy that gives you that lift. These foods also contain a stimulant called caffeine. Caffeine jolts your brain, keeping you alert and focused. In larger amounts, it can make you nervous and jittery. The government does not regulate foods that contain caffeine. It is therefore a legal stimulant.

Other stimulants affect the brain so powerfully and dangerously and unpredictably that

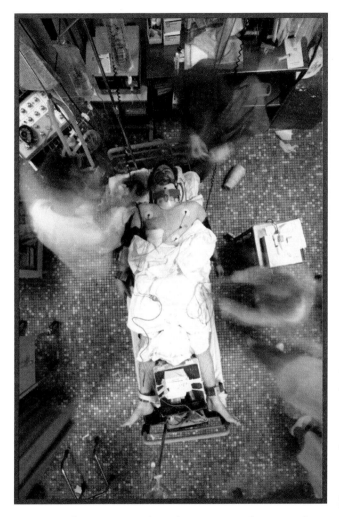

they are illegal. One such class of stimulants are amphetamines, including methamphetamine, commonly known as speed. Speed can produce in its users powerful feelings of alertness, courage, and incredible strength. Some users think that speed will make them more interesting and will solve all of their problems. But in the end, speed can kill.

Unfortunately, the use of speed among young people has increased during the 1990s. Speed is cheap to manufacture. It is sometimes called the poor person's cocaine. But it has also become one of the favorite drugs of suburban middle-class teenagers. In 1993, speed-related admissions to hospital emergency rooms increased by 61 percent over the previous year. In San Francisco and San Diego in 1992 and 1993, deaths from speed overdoses increased by 50 percent. A 1994 study by the University of Michigan found that 16 percent of the nation's high school seniors had tried speed. In 1998, commenting on an epidemic of crank use (crank is a form of speed) in Billings, Montana, *Time* magazine said, "People are losing everything to crank, their families, their jobs, their homes, their bank accounts, and, perhaps irretrievably, their minds." Amphetamine-type stimulants "grew more strongly than any other illicit substance in the 1990s," reported the United Nations' International Drug Control Program.

This is a speed epidemic, and maybe you or someone you know is a part of it. It's time for a serious look at what speed does to the brain and the body. It isn't pretty, but you might as well face the truth now, before you find yourself depressed and confused and mumbling incoherently, or beating up one of your friends in a fit of rage, or shaking uncontrollably on a gurney in a hospital emergency room. Sooner or later, people who use a lot of speed find themselves in trouble, after the high fades and they no longer feel like Superman.

1 The Brain and Central Nervous System

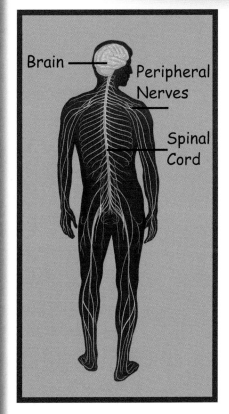

Brain — Peripheral Nerves

Spinal Cord

The brain is the organ of thought and consciousness, and through the central nervous system it controls and regulates all the other functions of your body. All thoughts, all memories, all sensations, and all decisions to act are processed by your brain. Your brain also controls all sorts of bodily functions that you never have to think about, like breathing and swallowing and blinking your eyes. Through its control of the body's glands, the brain regulates the release of chemicals that affect emotions, moods, and the body's metabolism. The brain controls everything and carries within itself everything that makes up your unique personality. Your brain, therefore, is you. Want to know what it would be like without a brain? That's a little hard to imagine, but think of what it is like when you are asleep and not dreaming. There is no sensation at all. An eternity of time passes in an instant because you are totally unaware of your surroundings, of your own existence. When your brain stops working, there is no you anymore, and indeed, this is one medical definition of death.

The brain doesn't have to stop working completely to cause you problems. As we shall see, when it is saturated with drugs or toxic chemicals, almost anything can happen. Your thoughts can become disconnected and irrational. Your memories can disappear. You can lose control of your emotions and moods. And sensations—sights, sounds, smells, and tastes, the things that clue you in to what is going on in the world outside of you—can become distorted and inaccurate and terrifying.

ANATOMY OF THE BRAIN

Your brain is a complicated piece of thinking machinery. It is divided into right and left hemispheres, and further sub-divided into sections—the forebrain, the midbrain, and the hindbrain. The forebrain is the biggest part of the brain and is sur-rounded by the cerebral cortex, often called the gray matter, where most of your conscious thinking and reasoning takes place. The midbrain, under-neath and within the fore-brain, interprets the signals that arrive from your sense organs and also controls some automatic movements. Once you decide to take a walk, for example, you don't have to con-stantly think about your balance or where to put your feet with each step because the midbrain does this for you. The hindbrain controls even more automatic functions, like

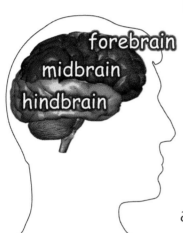

your breathing and your heartbeat, and from the base of the hindbrain your spinal cord carries signals along your central nervous system to and from all the parts of your body. Deep within your brain are other specialized organs like the thalamus and the hypothalamus that control the release of hormones that regulate your emotions and moods, your body temperature and blood pressure, your sex drive, and your appetite.

TRANSMITTING SIGNALS

What is important for us here is not the general anatomy of the brain but the fact that it is made up of hundreds of billions of separate nerve cells, or neurons, and that these neurons carry all the brain's signals. Each neuron has around its cell body a series of branching threads called dendrites, sometimes hundreds or even thousands of them, which pick up signals from other nerve cells. The signal is then transmitted down a long extension of the cell body called an axon, which also ends in a series of branching threads that pass the signal on to the dendrites of other neurons. In this way, passing from nerve cell to nerve cell, messages move back and forth from the brain to all parts of the body.

The brain's nerve cells are connected by axons. Axons are the conductors of nerve impulses, allowing for physiological activity.

The key to everything lies in the tiny spaces between these branching threads of the neurons, which are known as synapses, the contact points between nerve cells. These gaps are no more than a millionth of an inch wide. Because there are hundreds of billions of nerve cells in your brain, each with hundreds or thousands of dendrites, the total number of synaptic gaps within your brain actually exceeds the number of elementary particles in the known universe. How's that for complexity! No wonder you can think such complicated thoughts! No wonder it is so easy to get confused!

A signal is transmitted electrically, from one end of a

nerve cell to its other end, but when one nerve cell triggers another nerve cell, when a signal crosses the synapse, the signal is carried by chemicals known as neurotransmitters. Molecules of these chemicals actually travel across the synapse and stimulate the next nerve cell before they are reabsorbed by the neuron that released them. There are many chemical neurotransmitters that perform different functions, substances with names like acetylcholine, epinephrine and norepinephrine, dopamine, and serotonin. Actually, more often than not, these substances inhibit rather than stimulate other nerve cells and prevent signals

The point at which a nervous impulse passes from one neuron to another is called a synapse. The impulses, or signals, are carried by neurotransmitters.

from moving from neuron to neuron. If every time you tried to think more than a tiny fraction of those billions of nerve cells were activated, you would suffer a prolonged epileptic seizure, a kind of signal overload. So the purpose of many of these substances is to act as information traffic cops who keep order in the brain. And that's an important point to remember when we start to talk about drugs.

Drugs like methamphetamine—"speed" in street language—are also chemicals, chemicals that are absorbed into the brain tissue and can affect the way messages are carried across the synapses between nerve cells. Drugs can block the release of neurotransmitters or stimulate their release in greater amounts. Nerve cells can be fooled by such drugs into triggering signals when they are not supposed to. When this happens, anything goes! Your nerve cells are literally out of control, and the effects might include hallucinations and mood swings, irrational thinking, loss of control over movement, violent convulsions, unconsciousness, or death. Let's take a closer look now at what speed is and what it can do to your brain.

2 What Is Speed?

Speed is a term that is usually applied to a group of drugs collectively called amphetamines. Amphetamine, dextroamphetamine, and methamphetamine are similar in terms of chemical properties and the high or rush they produce. These drugs are strong stimulants. Stimulants commonly produce a sense of exhilaration,

Speed can lead to self-destructive actions, like this man trying to jump from a bridge.

enhanced self-esteem, a feeling of improved mental and physical performance, a reduced appetite, and relief from fatigue. Because they reverse the effects of fatigue and make you feel energized, these stimulants are also called uppers.

Also in this class of drugs are a number of amphetamine derivatives made in illegal labs and sold on the streets. These stimulants are sometimes identi- fied by initials or acronyms derived from their scientific names, and they usually have much stronger psycholog- ical effects and are more likely to cause all kinds of hal- lucinations. The most common of these drugs are trimethoxyamphetamine (known as TMA), 2,5- dimethoxyamphetamine, 4-methamphetamine (called "serenity," "tranquility," or "peace"), methoxyampheta- mine (STP), methylendioxyamphetamine (MDA), and paramethoxyamphetamine (PMA). They are all forms of speed.

Stimulants have many legitimate medical uses and are available in both prescription and nonprescription forms. Some stimulants dilate, or widen, the bronchial tubes in your lungs or the sinus passages in your nose, and they are found in medicines designed to reduce congestion caused by asthma, allergies, or colds. Other stimulants will suppress your appetite and increase your metabolism, the rate at which your body uses up energy, so they have been used successfully to help people lose weight. Because they are such powerful stimulants, some amphetamines are used to treat narcolepsy, a rare neurological disorder in which the sufferer falls into deep and uncontrollable sleeping spells. Some amphetamines are used to treat a condition called attention deficit hyperactivity disorder (ADHD), in which a person has trouble concentrating or staying focused on a particular task. This condition is usually treated with the stimulant methylphenidate, known commercially as Ritalin. There is some controversy about whether Ritalin is prescribed too often simply to control unruly kids.

Unfortunately, and precisely because they are such powerful stimulants, these drugs are often obtained illegally and used to get high, and in spite of their legitimate uses, they have become a serious medical problem.

EPHEDRINE AND AMPHETAMINE

The story of amphetamines begins with a substance called ephedrine. Ephedrine is the active ingredient in the Chinese herbal drug ma huang and has been used for centuries. In the 1920s, Dr. K. Chen of the Eli Lily Company extracted and identified ephedrine from ma huang. Ephedrine soon became an important drug in the treatment of asthma. But because the process of extracting the drug from the plant was difficult and the drug could not be synthesized in the lab, it was expensive and in short supply.

A few years later, a chemist named Gordon Alles tried to make synthetic ephedrine. Instead he made a new compound that he called amphetamine. Amphetamine had many of the same properties as ephedrine, and it quickly replaced ephedrine in the treatment of asthma.

Amphetamine was marketed under the name Benzadrine and was sold in nasal inhalers. The nasal inhalers rapidly gained popularity in the 1930s, not for their benefit to asthma sufferers but for their effects as stimulants. The use of nasal inhalers rapidly led to the widespread abuse of amphetamine.

Nasal inhalers used to dispense amphetamines, which rapidly led to their widespread abuse.

During World War II, amphetamines were given to soldiers to keep them alert and awake during long night watches or prolonged combat. More than 180 million pills were given out to soldiers during the war. After World War II, the abuse of amphetamines continued. Truckers used the drug to stay awake on long cross-country drives. To increase the effects of amphetamine, users began injecting the drug.

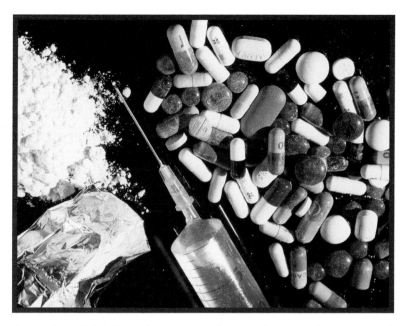

During the 1960s, the use of amphetamines as stimulants increased along with the abuse of many other drugs. As cocaine became more popular in the 1970s, the use of amphetamines began to drop. In the 1990s, however, the widespread availability of very cheap forms of speed, produced locally in underground labs, reversed that trend, and it is now one of the most popular stimulants among high school and college students who want to stay awake during long study sessions or for all-night parties.

Today, amphetamines are available in pills, capsules, powders, or in chunks or rocks resembling cocaine. The pills and capsules are taken orally, whereas the powders and rocks are either snorted through the nose or liquefied and injected into a vein. Some pharmaceutical amphetamines find their way to the street, where they are sold illegally, but most of the amphetamines available on the street today are illegally manufactured in underground speed labs and may contain dangerous impurities.

METHAMPHETAMINE

Methamphetamine is a more potent synthetic form of amphetamine. One type of methamphetamine, known as crystal meth or "ice," is sold on the streets in clear chunks, or rocks, and is heated and smoked in a manner similar to crack cocaine. Methamphetamine is also sold in the form of pills, capsules, and powders. The pills and capsules are taken orally, and the powders are either snorted, inhaled into the nose, or injected into a vein after some preparation.

WHERE SPEED COMES FROM

Speed—amphetamine and methamphetamine—is usually made in small, illegal labs called speed labs or meth labs. Underground meth labs exist in all areas of the United States and in many other countries. Meth labs are easy to construct from commonly available materials. A basic, small-scale meth lab requires the investment of only a few hundred dollars and can lead to enormous profits. But these profits come with high risk to the operators of the lab, their neighbors, and the drug users who patronize the lab. The chemicals commonly used in small speed labs include red phosphorus, hydrochloric acid, drain cleaner or lye, battery acid, lantern fuel, and antifreeze. Many of these substances are flammable, toxic, or caustic. Handling them can be very dangerous. When mixed together, they can also be explosive. Trained chemists take special precautions to protect themselves when they work with these chemicals. The operators of illegal speed labs seldom take the needed precautions.

A burned-out meth lab

Mishandling these kinds of chemicals can result in explosions that will destroy the meth lab and kill the operators of the lab and anyone else nearby. Because many meth labs are hidden in places such as old hotels, residential neighborhoods, and crowded trailer parks, there are usually large numbers of innocent people nearby. One drug enforcement agency estimates that about one out of every six meth labs catches fire and burns before it is discovered by authorities.

Some of these chemicals produce toxic or poisonous fumes that can overcome and kill the operator of the meth lab or escape from the lab and injure or kill someone nearby. Caustic chemicals used in the process of making speed can cause burns. If the caustic materials

The chemicals commonly used to manufacture speed are highly combustible. Therefore, when law enforcement officers make a raid on a speed lab, they must wear special protective gear.

are dumped illegally outside, anyone nearby can be affected. When law enforcement officers bust speed labs, they usually wear hazardous-material suits to protect themselves from these dangerous chemicals.

DANGERS TO THE ENVIRONMENT

Meth labs may also have a negative impact on the environment. Because so many hazardous chemicals are used in the production of speed and so much hazardous waste is produced, there is a problem with the storage and disposal of these materials. In legitimate industries, hazardous chemicals and wastes are properly stored or disposed of by incineration so that they do not pose a threat to the environment or people. Because meth labs are illegal, they do not follow these precautions.

The last thing a drug manufacturer wants is to advertise his presence by disposing dangerous chemicals in a legally authorized manner, complete with paperwork and government inspectors. Hazardous wastes from meth labs are often thrown out into garbage cans or Dumpsters, poured down the drain, dumped into a storm sewer, or poured out on the ground. Hazardous wastes dumped in the trash endanger anyone nearby and the people who collect the garbage. If the wastes are poured down the drain, they can cause explosions in the sewage system. If the wastes are disposed of either in storm sewers or on the ground, they can damage plant life and pollute nearby rivers and streams. When the chemicals find their way into nearby streams or rivers, this affects all of the fish and animals in the river as well as anyone who uses the water for a drinking system.

DANGERS TO DRUG USERS

Because speed is usually made in illegal labs, there is little or no quality control. The drugs may be contaminated by the different chemicals used in their production. Some of these contaminants can cause severe reactions in the user. Furthermore, the drugs can be cut, or diluted, with additives ranging from flour to caffeine. Sometimes the capsules or tablets contain no amphetamines at all—only caffeine.

Most dealers buy from other dealers or from meth labs. The speed passes through many different hands before it reaches the user. Dealers sell drugs for money and do not have the health and safety of their customers uppermost in their minds. Dealers will lie, cheat, steal, and sometimes even kill to protect their business and continue selling drugs. Because dealers are not afraid of breaking the law, buyers have no way of knowing what they are buying. Because the drug business operates outside of the law, there are no money-back guarantees. Anytime you buy drugs, you are taking a risk with your own health and safety.

3 How Is Speed Used?

Speed produces a feeling of euphoria and mental alertness. Taken orally, speed produces these effects within about fifteen to twenty minutes. If snorted, the effects begin in about three to five minutes. When speed is smoked or injected, the user experiences a rush almost immediately. Metabolism increases, as do blood pressure and pulse rate, and the user experiences a period of hyperactivity. He or she feels smart and assertive, as well as irritable and argumentative. As the effect wears off, the user crashes—that is, experiences a period of exhaustion and depression. At this point, the user feels a craving for the drug, wanting that high-energy feeling again to overcome the depression. Speed users also tend to use more and more of the drug over time as they develop a tolerance for it. When the body becomes accustomed to a drug, larger and larger doses must be taken to achieve the same high. These reactions determine the typical speed user's patterns of abuse.

BINGE AND CRASH

Some people may use speed only a few times, just to help them stay alert under stressful circumstances. But speed is a powerful and seductive drug, and many people quickly graduate to a pattern of abuse that is described by the phrase "binge and crash." During a binge-and-crash cycle, the abuser usually takes speed repeatedly and continuously over a period of time that may vary from a weekend to as long as a couple of weeks.

The binge-and-crash user begins the cycle by taking speed for four to sixteen hours. As the high wears off and fatigue and depression set in, the user will try to maintain the high by repeatedly taking more speed. This is the binge phase of the cycle. The user may try to maintain a high for as long as three to fifteen days. This includes a form of behavior known as tweaking.

Tweaking is a process by which a user takes small doses of speed continuously to try to maintain an alert state and to postpone the inevitable crash. This behavior may last for as long as two weeks, and during this time the user may

get no real sleep at all. He or she is also likely to be irritable and paranoid during this time. He or she may behave violently, especially if other substances such as alcohol are being abused. The user may also experience hallucinations and paranoia—an intense and irrational fear of almost everyone and everything around him or her. Tweaking can also result in suicidal feelings. The tweaker craves more speed but cannot re-create the initial high because his or her body is already awash in stimulants. This often produces intense feelings of frustration. The frustration may lead to unpredictable and violent or self-destructive actions.

Tweakers can appear normal at first glance—their eyes are clear, their speech is concise and coherent, and their movements are brisk—but if you look closer you can tell that something isn't right. Usually the user's eyes will be moving ten times faster than normal. The voice may have a slight quiver, and bodily movements are quick and jerky. Because of their unpredictable and possibly violent behavior, tweakers can be dangerous. Tweakers are often found at raves, or all-night parties. Tweakers are also often involved in traffic accidents and are responsible for many of the incidents classified as road rage. Tweakers may also take part in spur-of-the-moment crimes such as purse snatchings, muggings, or assaults for money to support their habit.

After the tweaking phase, the abuser finally crashes. If you are a tweaker, you will eventually find yourself mentally and physically exhausted, and you will usually sleep heavily for long periods. You may be fatigued and depressed for as long as three days following a binge. After this period of exhaustion, you may return for a while to a somewhat normal life with normal sleeping and eating patterns. You may feel weakened from the long binge, but you soon gain back your strength. After a few days or perhaps a week, you will be ready for another cycle of bingeing and crashing.

People who go through these long cycles of bingeing and crashing are called speed freaks. The main goal of a speed freak is to prevent a crash by tweaking, continuing to use more and more speed to keep from sinking into a state of depression, lethargy, and fatigue. Speed freaks basically try to stay high all the time. Because they consume such large amounts of speed, it is not uncommon for them to experience hallucinations. One common hallucination is the experience of crank bugs. The user feels as if bugs are crawling all over his or her body. He or she may violently scratch at the skin, which often leads to open wounds and ugly scars. If

31

you snort speed, your nasal passages can become burned and scarred. Other common signs of high-intensity speed use are extreme weight loss, pale skin, excessive sweating, body odor, and discolored teeth.

This severe skin lesion is the result of repeated and extreme scratching. Speed users often violently scratch at the skin when they hallucinate the presence of crank bugs.

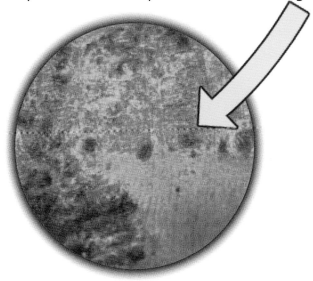

If you are able to break the binge-and-crash cycle, you will suffer from withdrawal symptoms. The symptoms of withdrawal are powerful depression and lethargy. Because the pleasure centers of the brain have been overstimulated and overworked by the drug, one symptom of withdrawal is the temporary inability to feel pleasure. These unpleasant feelings may cause the abuser to become suicidal. The desire to make these feelings go away is so strong that without help you are almost certain to want to get high again. For this reason, overcoming an addiction to speed is usually a complicated psychological process in which you must overcome your dependence on the drug for a sense of well-being.

4 How Does Speed Affect Your Brain?

Now we come to the scary part of this book. We're going to talk about what speed does to your brain, and through your brain, what it does to your body. We've already talked a little about the initial effects of the high caused by amphetamines. Speed stimulates the central nervous system and increases your heart rate and blood pressure,

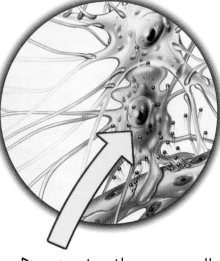

Drugs enter the nerve cells through blood vessels that feed oxygen to the cells.

Nerve cells are responsible for the fundamental functions of the brain. Damage to the nerve cells, a common result of speed use, can result in hyperactivity, paranoia, or violent and aggressive behavior.

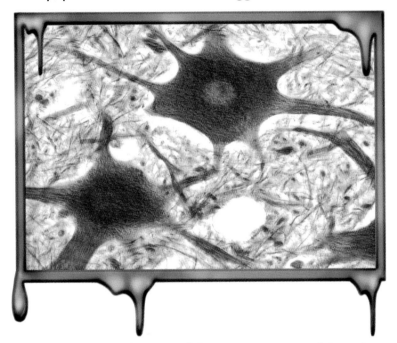

decreases your appetite, and increases your blood sugar levels. It also produces a variety of psychological effects—euphoria, hyperactivity, irritability, and aggressiveness. Speed causes these reactions because it interferes with the way neurons, or nerve cells, turn themselves on and off. As we have already described, a nerve cell "fires," that is, transmits a signal to another nerve cell, by releasing a chemical known as a neurotransmitter in the synapse, or gap, between those two cells. Then the neurotransmitter is reabsorbed and the triggering neuron quickly turns itself off. Speed interferes with the brain's ability to turn off this nervous stimulation. Nerve cells continue to stimulate other nerve cells in an uncontrollable chain reaction. Illnesses such as Parkinson's disease and epilepsy are also characterized by improperly firing nerve cells. Since the brain controls everything you do, the uncontrollable firing of nerve cells is bound to produce physiological changes and unusual behavior.

If you take a large enough dose of speed, or use speed frequently over a long period of time, you'll learn firsthand just how terrifying some of these changes can be. Hyperactivity, restlessness, moodiness, and irritability will evolve into extreme excitability, insomnia, anxiety, paranoia, and outright panic. That may be followed by mental confusion, violent and aggressive behavior, uncontrollable movements, and convulsions. Suicidal and homicidal tendencies may follow. You are going to become a walking time bomb of unbalanced and uncontrollable reactions, and your friends are going to avoid you like the plague. What exactly is happening to you?

NEUROTRANSMITTERS OUT OF CONTROL

The nerve cells that regulate your bodily functions respond to the neurotransmitters norepinephrine, epinephrine, dopamine, and serotonin. Each of these chemicals has a different molecular structure and stimulates a different response from the nerve cells.

Norepinephrine and epinephrine stimulate nerve cells associated with the body's "fight-or-flight" response to stress. The fight-or-flight response is part of the body's natural defense system. It prepares the body to protect itself by stimulating an aggressive reaction to stand and fight, or a fear reaction to run away from danger. These neurotransmitters cause the brain to focus its attention on the outside environment. They stimulate alertness to danger. They suppress your appetite and increase your heart rate to move blood quickly through the body. They also increase blood glucose levels for a quick boost of energy, and they dilate, or widen, your breathing tubes to increase the oxygen supply in your blood.

The cost of this increased mental and physical efficiency is a big increase in the amount of energy the body needs to consume. Because the body is not taking in food, it is converting fat into energy. This is why speed causes weight loss. Your body no longer craves food, hormone levels are at high levels, and your body temperature is raised. This condition allows the body to function much more efficiently. But increased efficiency

has its downside. You are really living on the edge, with the speed stimulating hyperactive reactions that may easily run out of control and produce the dramatic and violent symptoms we discussed previously. And this hyperactivity can't be sustained.

This state of heightened concentration and readiness for danger drains the body of energy. When the brain naturally invokes this response, it usually lasts no more than a couple of hours. Under normal circumstances, the body can quickly recover from this energy drain. But when the body is stimu-lated with speed, this heightened state of alertness can last for eighteen to twenty-four hours, or even for days or weeks if you continue tweaking to keep yourself high. This causes the body to draw deeply on its energy reserves. As these energy reserves are exhausted, the user eventually crashes. A crash requires sleep and food to help the body recover.

The neurotransmitter dopamine has a different func-tion. It causes a sense of pleasure and euphoria. It also controls the release of some hormones and affects your fine muscle control. The neurotransmitter serotonin is involved in the regulation of sleep and psychological moods. It also influences your body's ability to regulate temperature and control appetite. An increase in body tem-perature speeds up the chemical reactions that release the energy stored in the body's fat cells, so that serotonin makes more energy available for the body. This increased body temperature is dangerous, however, especially for athletes, because exercise only increases body temperature even more. If you were to raise your body temperature as high as 108 degrees Fahrenheit, you would suffer irre-versible brain damage, and you might even die.

THE IMMEDIATE PHYSICAL DANGERS OF SPEED

Of course, there is no predicting what kind of physical dangers you might face when your mind has been taken over by feelings of paranoia and panic. Speed freaks have been known to do some pretty weird things. But there are many more immediate dangers, especially if you overdose on speed. Because speed increases your blood pressure and heart rate, it can cause a heart attack or stroke. In low doses, speed would probably

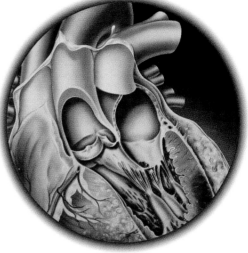

This heart shows extreme muscle damage, probably the result of a fatal heart attack. There is evidence of extensive cell death and scarring as well as blood clots.

cause this only if you had a preexisting heart problem or weakened arteries. But in larger doses, a heart attack or a stroke is a real risk. Remember that when speed is purchased on the street, its purity is not known. As a result, it

THE EFFECTS OF METHAMPHETAMINE

The National Drug and Alcohol Treatment Referral Routing Service recently compiled this summary of the dangerous health effects of methamphetamine:

Short-Term Effects

increased alertness
uncontrollable movements
sense of well-being
violent behavior
paranoia
insomnia (inability to sleep)
intense high

impaired speech
increased heart rate
dry, itchy skin
convulsions
loss of appetite
rise in body temperature
acne, sores, numbness

Effects on the Mind

disturbed sleep
false sense of confidence
    and power
excessive excitation
delusions of grandeur
excessive talking

lack of interest in friends,
    food, sex
panic, anxiety, nervousness
aggressive or violent behavior
moodiness and irritability
severe depression

Withdrawal Symptoms

severe cravings
depression
insomnia
itching

restlessness
sweats
mental confusion
violent behavior

Long-Term Effects

fatal kidney and lung disorders
depression

brain damage
hallucinations

is difficult to estimate the strength of the dose you are taking. This increases the likelihood of a high dose or even an overdose.

An overdose from speed can happen in two different ways. A single large dose may put you over the edge, or you may take repeated doses by tweaking until toxic levels are reached. Either way, the result is the same. Few people survive an overdose of speed without immediate medical attention. When speed reaches a toxic level in the blood, you may experience seizures, convulsions, or a fatal elevation of body temperature, in addition to the possibility of a heart attack or stroke. Even when death does not occur, a speed overdose usually leaves the victim with severe damage to the brain or heart.

THE LONG-TERM EFFECTS OF SPEED

There are many dangers associated with the long-term use of speed. The use of speed can cause a mental illness similar to paranoid schizophrenia. Malnutrition due to high energy usage and appetite suppression is common among speed freaks. The generally weakened state of the body from lack of rest and poor diet makes it more susceptible to disease. Injecting speed and sharing needles expose users to infections and blood-borne diseases such as AIDS and hepatitis. Blood vessels may become blocked, increasing the possibility of a heart attack later in life. Finally, because of heightened irritability and aggression, speed users may commit crimes or cause injuries to innocent people.

The use of speed during pregnancy can affect an unborn baby. Because speed travels through the blood-stream, it can pass through the placenta to the unborn child. Speed can cause birth defects such as heart defects, cleft palates, and physical and mental disorders. It may also produce a baby addicted to speed who will suffer withdrawal symptoms from the moment of birth.

Other possible long-term effects from speed use include fatal kidney or

lung disorders, liver damage, brain damage, permanent psychological disorders, a disorganized lifestyle, a restricted social life, chronic hallucinations, and chronic depression.

So speed is really one drug that you don't want to fool with. It wreaks havoc with the switching centers of your brain, and it can turn you into a gibbering idiot in no time at all. It can scramble your personality until you have no notion of who you are anymore. Any cop who has had to deal on his or her beat with an out-of-control speed freak can tell you stories of teens who thought they were being pursued by demons and probably tried to kill themselves to escape these imaginary enemies. And drug counselors will tell you that it may take weeks of detoxification with powerful antipsychotic drugs just to get to the point where they can reason with speed abusers. Amphetamines are really powerful drugs, and the depression and inability to experience pleasurable feelings that come with withdrawal make kicking the speed habit especially hard. All too many speed users don't wake up to the dangers of this drug until they find themselves in a hospital emergency room. Don't take that gamble. Don't lose your mind.

GLOSSARY

amphetamines Powerful synthetic stimulants, a number of drugs popularly known as speed.

binge A period of intense use of a stimulant, which may last from three to fifteen days and is followed by a period of exhaustion known as a crash.

crash To come down off stimulants and experience a period of physical and mental exhaustion.

ephedrine Natural stimulant found in the Chinese herb ma huang.

ice A smokable form of methamphetamine.

methamphetamine The most powerful of the synthetic stimulants, also known as speed.

neurotransmitter A chemical that transmits signals between nerve cells.

rush The sudden feeling of euphoria associated with smoking or injecting speed.

speed Stimulants such as amphetamine or methamphetamine.

speed freak A habitual speed user.

tolerance The body's ability to get used to, or become less responsive to, a drug, requiring larger doses to get the same effect.

FOR MORE INFORMATION

In the United States

Families Anonymous
P.O. Box 3475
Culver City, CA 90231
(800) 736-9805

Narcotics Anonymous
World Service Office
P.O. Box 9999
Van Nuys, CA 91409
(818) 773-9999
Web site: http://www.na.org

National Clearinghouse for Alcohol
    and Drug Information
Center for Substance Abuse
    Prevention
5600 Fishers Lane, Rockwall II
Rockville, MD 20857
(301) 443-0365
Web site: http://www.health.org

The National Institute on
    Drug Abuse
National Institutes of Health (NIH)
Bethesda, MD 20892
Web site: http://www.nida.nih.gov

The Partnership for a Drug-Free
    America
Lexington Avenue, 16th Floor
New York, NY 10174
Web site:
http://www.drugfreeamerica.org

In Canada

Family Services Youth Detox
    Program
4305 St. Catherine Street
Vancouver, BC V5V 4M4
(604) 872-4349

Narcotics Anonymous
P.O. Box 5700, Depot A
Toronto, ON M5W 1N9
(416) 691-9519

FOR FURTHER READING

Clayton, Lawrence. *Amphetamines and Other Stimulants.* Rev. ed. New York: The Rosen Publishing Group, 1997.

Moser, Leslie E. *Crack, Cocaine, Methamphetamine, and Ice.* Waco, TX: Multi-Media Productions, Inc., 1990.

Nagle, Jeanne. *Everything You Need to Know About Drug Addiction.* New York: The Rosen Publishing Group, 1999.

Wesson, Donald R. *Crack and Ice: Treating Smokeable Stimulant Abuse.* Center City, MN: Hazelden Educational Materials, 1992.

INDEX

CREDITS

About the Author

Allan B. Cobb is a freelance science writer who lives in central Texas. He has written books, articles, radio scripts, and educational materials concerning different aspects of science. When not writing about science, he enjoys traveling, camping, hiking, and exploring caves.

Photo Credits

Series Design

Laura Murawski

Layout

Cynthia Williamson